W9-BYY-572

DISCARD

CLINTON, IOWA

PRESIDENTIAL LIBRARIES™

JOHN F. KENNEDY
LIBRARY AND MUSEUM

Amy Margaret

The Rosen Publishing Group's
PowerKids Press™

New York

CLINTON PUBLIC LIBRARY
CLINTON, IOWA
52732

For Benjamin Luke and Grace Kathryn

Acknowledgment: The author would like to thank Jim Wagner, museum specialist for the JFK Library and Museum, for his invaluable assistance on this project.

Published in 2004 by The Rosen Publishing Group, Inc.
29 East 21st Street, New York, NY 10010

Copyright © 2004 by The Rosen Publishing Group, Inc.

All rights reserved. No part of this book may be reproduced in any form without permission in writing from the publisher, except by a reviewer.

First Edition

Editor: Joanne Riethoff
Book Design: Maria E. Melendez
Book Layout: Eric DePalo

Photo credits: Cover, title page, pp. 4, 6, 7, 9 (top and bottom left), 10, 13 (bottom), 15 (bottom), 17 (top left, right), 21, 22 courtesy of John F. Kennedy Library; pp. 5, 9 (right) Robert Schoen/ John F. Kennedy Library; pp. 8, 12 courtesy of Joel Benjamin/John F. Kennedy Library; p. 11 (top) © Robert Lackenbach/Black Star/TimePix; p. 11 (bottom) © The Peace Corps; pp. 13 (top), 15 (top), 18, 20 courtesy of Cecil Stoughton, White House/ John F. Kennedy Library; p. 14 © Bettman/Stanley Tretick, 1963/CORBIS; p. 16 courtesy of Abbie Rowe, National Park Service/John F. Kennedy Library; p. 17 (bottom left) courtesy of Donald Dietz/John F. Kennedy Library; p. 19 (top) Bettman/CORBIS; p. 19 (bottom) AP/Wide World Photos.

Margaret, Amy.
  John F. Kennedy Library and Museum / by Amy Margaret.
     p. cm. — (Presidential libraries)
  Includes bibliographical references and index.
  ISBN 0-8239-6269-5 (library binding)
  1. John F. Kennedy Library and Museum—Juvenile literature. 2. Kennedy, John F. (John Fitzgerald), 1917–1963—Archives—Juvenile literature. 3. Presidents—United States—Archives—Juvenile literature. 4. Kennedy, John F. (John Fitzgerald), 1917–1963—Museums—Massachusetts—Boston—Juvenile literature. 5. Kennedy, John F. (John Fitzgerald), 1917–1963—Juvenile literature. 6. Presidents—United States—Biography—Juvenile literature. [1. John F. Kennedy Library and Museum. 2. Kennedy, John F. (John Fitzgerald), 1917–1963. 3. Presidents.] I. Title.
  E838.5.K49 M37 2003
  973.922'092—dc21

                    2001006661

Manufactured in the United States of America

CONTENTS

8/25/05

Randolph   13.60 M J

228 6919

A VISIT TO THE JFK LIBRARY

The JFK Library and Museum is the fourth presidential library in the United States. A presidential library holds papers and historical materials from a specific president's time in office. When a president leaves office, the National Archives and Records Administration (NARA) receives this material. The NARA is in charge of all the presidential libraries.

The John F. Kennedy Library and Museum opened to the public in 1979. It is located next to Dorchester Bay, in Boston, Massachusetts.

The goals of the library and museum are to encourage learning about both the U.S. government and service to the community and the country. The museum also celebrates the **accomplishments** of John F. Kennedy, who is referred to as JFK. Visitors can feel as if they are at the 1960 **Democratic Convention** as they walk through an area that is set up like the convention room. They can also see what the Oval Office looked like when JFK used it during his White House years, from 1961 to 1963.

I. M. Pei designed the John F. Kennedy Library and Museum. The library is 125 feet (38 m) high. The upper floors are used for offices, for research, and for storage. The lower floors and the museum area have two small theaters that show short films. Visitors can view old television videos, historic photographs, and other objects from the library's collection.

THE PRESIDENT AS A CHILD

Jack (right) *is shown here with his older brother Joe Jr. (left) in Hyannis Port, Massachusetts, in 1925. Jack and Joe Jr. used to compete with each other. Joe Jr. was a very good student. Jack didn't do as well, except in his favorite subjects, history and English.*

John Fitzgerald Kennedy, who was called Jack, was the second-oldest boy of nine children. He was born on May 29, 1917, to Rose and Joseph Kennedy. Jack and his eight brothers and sisters grew up in Brookline, near Boston, Massachusetts. In school Jack's favorite subjects were history and English. Library visitors can see a copy of one of his report cards.

Jack's interest in history continued when he entered Harvard University, Cambridge, Massachusetts, in 1936. Jack's father and Joe Jr. had gone to Harvard, too. Jack loved to swim, so he joined the swim team. Later his swimming skills helped him become a hero.

Jack didn't always do well in school. Visitors can see these comments on one of Jack's papers. Even though Jack got a good mark on this paper, his teacher still wrote that his work was "badly written."

UAV 453.239

REPORT ON THESIS FOR DISTINCTION

Name of Candidate KENNEDY, J.F. '40

Title of Thesis APPEASEMENT AT MUNICH

Grade *Magna cum laude*

(Indicate whether rank is *summa cum laude*, *magna cum laude*, or *cum laude*, or not of distinction grade (C, D or E). Use *plus* or *minus*, where necessary.)

Remarks (Please indicate more fully the special excellences or defects of the thesis.)

Badly written; but a laborious, interesting and intelligent discussion of a difficult question

Henry A. Yeomans (Signature)

Jack stands with seven of his brothers and sisters in Hyannis Port, Massachusetts, in 1928. From bottom left to top right, they are Jean, Robert, Patricia, Eunice, Kathleen, Rosemary, Jack, and Joe Jr.

THE ROAD TO THE PRESIDENCY

In 1943, JFK's boat was struck by the Japanese in the South Pacific. Two men died, and the rest had to swim 3 ½ miles (6 km). JFK swam to shore carrying an injured man. He carved a message on a coconut. Two natives brought it to a harbor 40 miles (64 km) away. The coconut is shown above in the Man of the Sea exhibit, which ran from June 3, 2000 to April 30, 2001.

JFK graduated from Harvard in 1940. He was accepted into the U.S. Navy in September 1941, two months before the United States entered **World War II**.

In 1943, JFK's **PT boat** was struck by the Japanese in the South Pacific. Even though he was injured, he led his men to safety and became a hero. He eventually got malaria, a serious illness, and was sent home. Some items used by JFK in the war are exhibited at the library.

In 1946, JFK got involved in politics and won a seat in the **House of Representatives**. In 1952, he ran for the **Senate** and won. In 1960, JFK decided to run for president of the United States. He was **nominated** for president in July.

Here JFK is shown in his white Navy uniform as a young man. In 1943, he was made a lieutenant in the Navy.

This is the PT 109 exhibit at the library. Among the items shown here are the coconut that JFK carved a message on, the flag from his boat, and his uniform.

JFK is shown here in his PT boat. This photograph was taken in 1943.

KENNEDY AROUND THE WORLD

Founded in 1985, the JFK Library Corps is a service group made up of Boston youth, from ages 11 to 18. Similar to the Peace Corps, the Library Corps members volunteer their time to help people in their community. This organization was named for JFK, shown here giving a speech on March 13, 1961.

As president, JFK had a desire to reach out to other countries around the world. In 1961, he developed the **Peace Corps**, which still exists today. The Peace Corps is made up of people who are trained to help **underdeveloped** countries. These people **volunteer** to live and work with the locals of the country. They build houses, teach, and farm.

JFK visited many countries, such as Austria and Germany. He spoke in West Berlin after the **Berlin Wall** was built in 1961. JFK ended his speech about freedom by saying, "I am a native Berliner." It was said that in German he mistakenly said, "I am a jelly doughnut," but this is not really true.

West Berlin was just one of the many places where JFK went overseas. Here we see him making his now famous speech to the crowd in West Berlin in June 1963. Robert Lackenbach was there to take this photograph.

When the Peace Corps was created, about 5,000 young people quickly signed up to help overseas. During JFK's three years in office, volunteers worked in 47 countries.

SPACE RACE

In 1957, the former Soviet Union sent *Sputnik*, the world's first **satellite**, into space. In April 1961, the Soviet Union put a person in space. The U.S. space program entered the **space race** that year. American astronaut John Glenn orbited Earth three times in 1961, in the spacecraft *Friendship 7*. After this JFK announced that the U.S. space program would land a man on the Moon and return him to Earth by 1970. On July 20, 1969, American Neil Armstrong became the first person to set foot on the Moon.

An exhibit at the museum shows items related to space travel. It features a copy of Glenn's 1962 space suit and materials from his latest space voyage in 1998.

The United States was shocked that the Soviet Union had been the first of the two countries to explore outer space. The space race began. With each country trying to outdo the other, they both were able to make many advancements in their space programs. This period in history is shown in the John Glenn and the Space Program exhibit.

JFK, Jackie, and members of JFK's White House staff watch their television on May 5, 1961, waiting for news about astronaut Alan Shepard, the first American in space. He flew on Mercury 3.

John Glenn landed back on Earth only about 5 hours after he took off on February 20, 1962. JFK is shown here with John Glenn in Cape Canaveral on February 23, 1962. They are looking at Friendship 7.

A FAMILY MAN

In the White House, Caroline and John Jr. played with their father every morning before he went down to the Oval Office. In addition to spending time with their father every morning, the children got to be with him during the day, too. JFK is seen here with his son, John Jr., who is peeking out from under his father's desk. This picture was taken on October 14, 1963.

JFK met Jacqueline Bouvier at a dinner party given by a friend of JFK's father. They married about a year later, on September 12, 1953. In November 1957, Jackie gave birth to Caroline Bouvier Kennedy. Their second child, John Jr., was born in November 1960. Caroline was three years old and John Jr. was about two months old when the family moved into the White House.

People all around the country were interested in the Kennedy family. Members of JFK's family were powerful people in the government. As the Kennedy family grew, they were sometimes called American royalty. The Kennedy family was very popular with the public.

Caroline and John Jr. are shown here playing with their father in the Oval Office on November 11, 1963. Many snapshots and formal photographs can be seen at the JFK Library.

Jackie tried to create a family home in the White House. She did not allow photographs to be taken without her permission. This photograph of the Kennedy family was taken on August 4, 1962, at Hyannis Port, Massachusetts.

THE FIRST LADY

Jacqueline Bouvier was born in 1929. She grew up in a wealthy Catholic family, as did JFK. She graduated from George Washington University in 1951. Her first job was for a Washington newspaper.

Once the Kennedy family was in the White House, Jackie turned her attention to the mansion. Her first trip to the White House had been as a tourist in 1941. She was disappointed in the lack of historical objects and furniture. Her goal as First Lady was to remodel the White House with items from the time periods reflected in the various rooms.

Jackie chose the architect and the location for the JFK Library and Museum. Jackie died of cancer in 1994.

Here Jackie is shown on June 28, 1962, opening the Treaty Room, one of the rooms in the White House that was redone. In February 1962, CBS and NBC showed an hour-long television special called "A Tour of the White House with Mrs. John F. Kennedy." About one-third of the country tuned in to see the rooms of the White House.

This is the Oval Office exhibit at the JFK Museum. JFK used this office when he signed official papers and when he met with important people.

This photograph shows one of the hallways in the White House that Jackie redecorated. She restored the rooms and corridors of the White House.

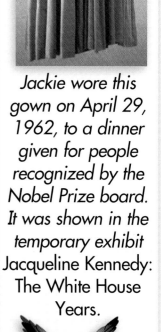

Jackie wore this gown on April 29, 1962, to a dinner given for people recognized by the Nobel Prize board. It was shown in the temporary exhibit Jacqueline Kennedy: The White House Years.

NOVEMBER 22, 1963

After visiting Texas cities San Antonio, Houston, and Fort Worth, JFK and his staff flew to Dallas on the morning of November 22. Here we see Jackie greeting people after they arrived.

President and Mrs. Kennedy traveled to Texas on November 21, 1963. JFK was hoping to win Texas's vote when he ran for reelection in 1964.

About 12:00 P.M. the next day, he, his wife, Texas governor John Connally, and Mrs. Connally were driven through Dallas. Just a few minutes away from where they were going, both President Kennedy and Governor Connally were shot. Connally recovered, but Kennedy's wounds were too severe, and he died.

At the JFK Museum, the final exhibit plays a video of Walter Cronkite announcing the news of JFK's **assassination**. Walter Cronkite was a news announcer from 1962 to 1981.

This picture was taken shortly before the shots were fired on November 22, 1963. Lee Harvey Oswald was arrested for the shooting but was assassinated soon after. There are still unanswered questions about who was responsible for JFK's murder.

This picture was taken at the funeral for JFK. Jackie is dressed in black, JFK's brother Bobby is to her left, Caroline is to her right, and John Jr. is saluting his father's coffin. This picture was taken on November 25, 1963, John Jr.'s birthday.

SPECIAL EXHIBITS

One of the museum's small theaters shows a short film about the Cuban missile crisis. The Cuban missile crisis was a time when the Soviet Union supported Fidel Castro, the leader of Cuba, and supplied Cuba with missiles. Shown above is JFK (left) meeting with his advisers on October 29, 1962, to talk about the crisis.

It is a tradition for leaders of countries to give gifts to one another when they meet. Among the gifts given to JFK and his wife is a crystal vase from New Ross, Ireland. The vase shows an Irish home, a ship, and the White House. JFK's grandfather, Patrick Kennedy, left New Ross in 1848, to start a new life in Boston. This vase shows the Kennedy family history.

The museum features exhibits important to Kennedy's White House years. One exhibit is about the television address JFK gave on the fight against **segregation**, in the early 1960s. There are also pictures of JFK with leaders of this fight, such as Martin Luther King Jr.

Egyptian president Gamal Abdel Nasser gave Mrs. Kennedy this 4,000-year-old Egyptian statue to thank her for helping to save the temples in the Nile Valley in Egypt.

THE PRESIDENT'S LEGACY

In 1989, the John F. Kennedy Foundation formed the Profile in Courage Award. It is given yearly to recognize political courage. The award consists of $25,000 and a silver lantern (above) designed by Edwin Schlossberg and made by Tiffany & Company.

The JFK Library and Museum is certainly one of the best memorials to JFK, with its many collections and exhibits about his life. Many other buildings are named for him, including the Kennedy Space Center in Florida.

In 1955, JFK wrote *Profiles in Courage*, a book about senators who had courage and who were great leaders. This book won the **Pulitzer Prize** in 1957. Copies of *Profiles in Courage* are available at the JFK Library.

The JFK Library and Museum shows the courage John F. Kennedy had throughout his life. The library and museum help others to find this courage and desire for excellence in themselves.

GLOSSARY

accomplishments (uh-KOM-plish-ments) Things a person finishes well.

assassination (uh-sa-sin-AY-shun) When an important or famous person is murdered.

Berlin Wall (BER-lin WAHL) A wall put up after World War II that separated East Berlin from West Berlin. This wall was torn down in 1989.

Democratic Convention (deh-moh-KRA-tik kun-VEN-shun) The meeting in which the democratic party chooses a presidential candidate.

House of Representatives (HOWS UV reh-prih-ZEN-tuh-tivz) A part of Congress, the law-making part of the U.S. government.

nominated (NAH-mih-nayt-ed) To have gotten picked for something.

Peace Corps (PEES COR) A group of volunteers that helps underdeveloped countries.

PT boat (PEE TEE BOHT) A light, fast boat that is used to launch torpedoes.

Pulitzer Prize (PYOO-lit-zur PRYZ) An award given to authors for their accomplishments in writing.

satellite (SA-til-eyet) A human-made or natural object that orbits another object.

segregation (seh-gruh-GAY-shun) When people are separated because of their race.

Senate (SEH-nit) A law-making part of the U.S. government.

space race (SPAYS RAYS) The competition in the 1950s and 1960s between the United States and the Soviet Union to explore space.

underdeveloped (uhn-dur-dih-VEH-lupt) To not be so advanced in areas such as agriculture and industry.

volunteer (vah-luhn-TEER) To work without getting paid.

World War II (WURLD WOR TOO) A war fought between the United States, Great Britain, and Russia, and Germany, Japan, and Italy from 1939 to 1945.

CLINTON PUBLIC LIBRARY
CLINTON, IOWA

INDEX

PRIMARY SOURCES

Pages 5–10, 12–13, 15–18, 20–22. *Pictures were obtained directly from the John F. Kennedy Library and Museum.* **Page 11 (bottom).** *This is a recent photograph obtained from the Peace Corps.*

WEB SITES

Due to the changing nature of Internet links, PowerKids Press has developed an online list of Web sites related to the subject of this book. This site is updated regularly. Please use this link to access the list:
www.powerkids.links.com/pl/jfklm/